Marlene

ACKNOWLEDGMENTS

I would first thank Harry Evans, President and Publisher, Random House Trade Group, who first had the idea of having me collect this material on Dietrich. Also I want to thank my assistant, Crosby Coughlin, whose indefatigable energy and enthusiasm made this project possible. My thanks to Maryam Mohit, Assistant Editor at Random House, for her thoughtful advice, and then my thanks to Maria Bavosa, who supervised brilliantly the production of this book. My thanks to Gar Lillard of Lab One, who produced the photographic prints to perfection. And, finally, to Denise Otis, whose understanding helped me edit the texts.

Marlene

AN INTIMATE PHOTOGRAPHIC MEMOIR

BY ALEXANDER LIBERMAN

Random House

Photographs pp. 34–35, 120, courtesy of Archive Photo; pp. 20–21, 119, courtesy of Bison; pp. 26–27, 32–33, courtesy of Christophe Collection; front endpaper courtesy of Culver pictures; pp. 12–13, 14–15, courtesy of Edimedia; pp. 22, 29, courtesy of Everett Collection; pp. 18–19, courtesy of Harlingue-Viollet; pp. 8–9, 16–17, courtesy of Kipa; pp. 10–11, 24–25, 30–31, courtesy of Kobal Collection; p. 6, courtesy of the Museum of Modern Art; back endpaper courtesy of Parallel; p. 28, courtesy of Photofest

Hal Leonard Music Publishing Corporation and Apollo-Verlag Paul Lincke, Berlin: Three pages of sheet music to *"Lilli Marlene"*, German lyric by Hans Leip, English lyric by Tommie Connor, Music by Norbert Schultze. Copyright 1940 by Apollo-Verlag Paul Lincke, Berlin. Copyright renewed. English lyric copyright 1944 by Peter Maurice Music Co. Ltd. Published by permission of the Music Publishing House: Apollo-Verlag Paul Lincke, Berlin. Sole distributor for the USA and Mexico: Edward B. Marks Music Company.

Library of Congress Cataloging-in-Publication Data

Liberman, Alexander
    Marlene: an intimate photographic memoir/Alexander Liberman.

        p.   cm.
    ISBN 0-679-42086-X
    1. Dietrich, Marlene—Portraits.   2. Entertainers—Germany—
Portraits.   I. Title.
PN2658. D5M38 1992
791.43'028'092—dc20
[B]   92-50548

Manufactured in Italy
98765432
First Edition

Front endpaper   1930—Lola-Lola in *The Blue Angel*

Back endpaper   1930—In *The Blue Angel*, the coy
                        seduction of Emil Jannings.

CONTENTS

Marlene

THE
LEGEND

On the following pages I have selected some images from Marlene's great films that stay in our memory as unique incarnations of feminine beauty and seduction.

Marlene is a block of ice, and extraordinarily photogenic. Here she has not yet been transformed by Hollywood's glamour. (*Morocco*, 1930)

Preceding page, Marlene with American troops in Germany, 1945.

Marlene embodies the cold, strong woman, the impassive object of desire who will spit on human weakness. But at the end of *Morocco* we see her forsake her previous life to follow her French Legionnaire into the desert. (*Morocco*, with Gary Cooper, 1930)

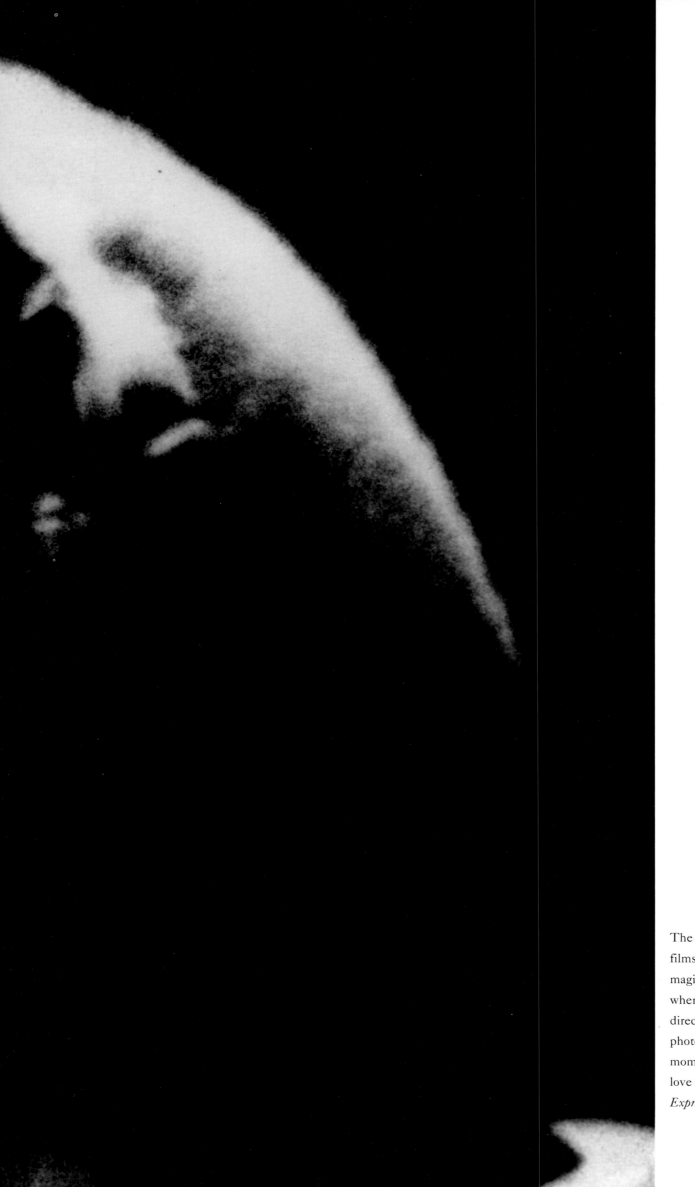

The one time that
films captured the
magic in Marlene's face was
when von Sternberg was her
director, for each of his
photographs of her is a
moment of devotion to his
love object. (*Shanghai
Express*, 1932)

13

Shanghai Express perhaps
epitomizes von Sternberg's
ability to glorify Marlene's
beauty through the
use of light and shadow.
(*Shanghai Express*,
with Clive Brook, 1932)

Her lavish costumes gave
her a sense of otherworldliness;
her impassive face emerges
from the fantasy of feathers and
glitter. With Cary Grant.
(*Blonde Venus*, 1932)

Marlene knew how
she looked best; the
shadow under her
nose gives it a sharper line.
(*The Scarlet Empress*, 1934)

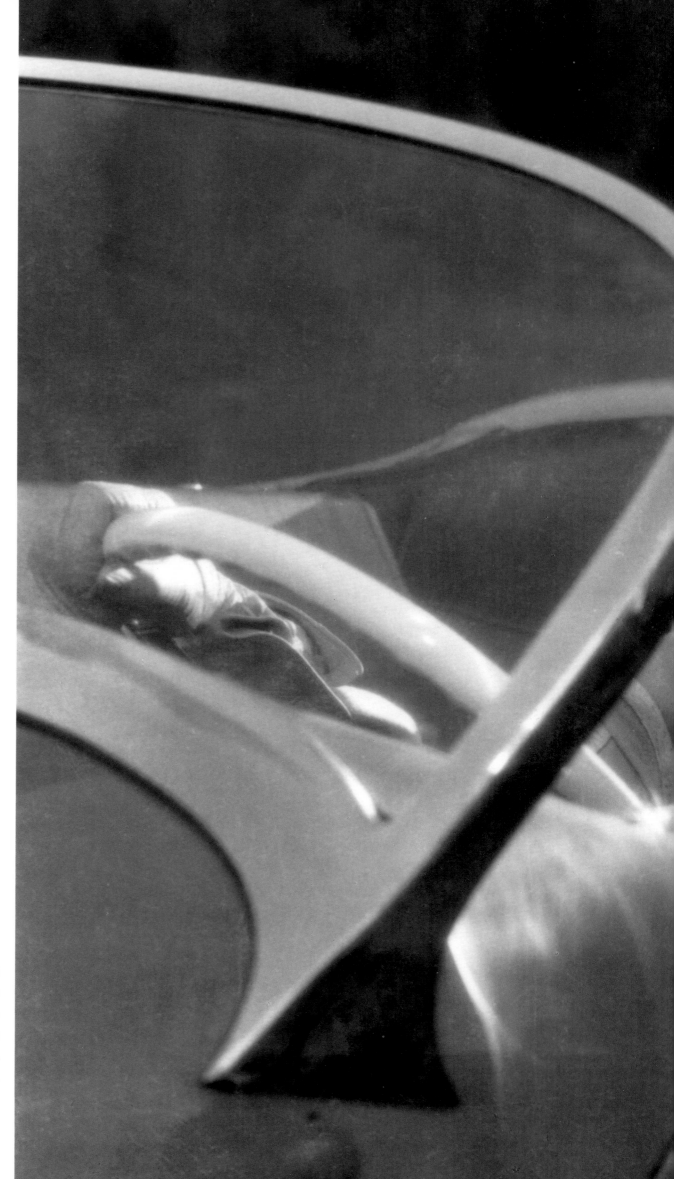

Marlene provided a field day for costume designers to try their most bravura inventions. The hat she wears is nonsensical, but it frames her face with mystery. (*Desire*, 1936)

She understood how to use light to enhance her steely features. (*The Garden of Allah*, 1936)

What Marlene projected
was a curious mixture of coldness
and sexuality. The men in
her films are generally
portrayed as defenseless in
her sexual presence. (*The
Garden of Allah*, with Charles
Boyer, 1936)

Given her statuesque, waxlike quality, Marlene was the ideal body on which to drape fetishistic garments—feathers, furs, sparkles. (*Morocco*, 1930)

Marlene enjoyed wearing uniforms, especially men's tails, which brought out the most alluring proportions of her long legs. The toppers and the giant boutonniere in her lapel provoke a touch of mockery at herself and the world. (*Seven Sinners*, 1940, left; *Morocco*, 1930, right)

In the role of Jamilla,
Marlene lent her body to all
erotic fantasies. The face,
her unalterable mask, remains
beyond the director's whim.
(*Kismet*, 1944)

The one time she made a film with the great love of her life, Jean Gabin, she ended up portraying a French society lady, not at all in her character. She wanted to please Gabin, and he had very conventional desires.

(*Martin Roumagnac*, 1946)

Here, in one of her last films, her face still unchanging. (*Witness for the Prosecution*, with Charles Laughton, 1957)

Marlene
MY FRIEND

I was seventeen and in Paris when I first saw Marlene in *The Blue Angel*. Every detail of her intensely erotic costume, calculated to titillate old Jannings, inflamed all of us: the indescribable rasping voice, the haunting theme tune, the black garters two exclamation points on the white fleshy thighs. To make the pleasure more unendurable we watched the film over and over again. We reveled in the pleasure and pain of her consummate teasing, the magnetic sexual allure followed by the tongue-in-cheek scorn for all desire, male and female. She was at once the yielding female and the dominant male. The contrast between feminine frills and the masculine rigidity of the top hat she affected added to the male-female interplay she projected. Later she was the first woman to appear in public wearing pants: a real man's suit. The fetish, the top hat, stayed with her throughout her life onstage. Never worn straight, always at a cheeky angle, it was constantly provocative and impertinent. Even her berets had an aggressive tilt.

This early Marlene's mischievous androgyny stamped her for life. When I came to know her in the early fifties, she was no longer a sex kitten, but she had not lost that incandescence of earthiness and spirit, and she never did. She was eternal. Her eyes were large, irises pale and Prussian. They could still dart sparks of contempt, as in *The Blue Angel*. One of my ineradicable memories is of seeing her dance with a partner she cared for. This was at a charity dance in a restaurant. She wore a soft black dress, a then-fashionable black straw hat. . . but the amazingly graceful, rhythmic fluidity of her whole body made an extraordinary sensual imprint on all who watched. The movement had a feline, animal power, a hint of what amorous possession could be.

Yet we also saw the other Marlene, the German housewife. The professional glamour would disappear as she played the servant. Deep in her there seemed to be a mysterious pull to abase herself, a masochistic urge to be humbled, to be the debased servant of whoever loved her. Marlene is also Maria-Magdalena; this was her second name and it was prophetic of her behavior in private life. The mythic Magdalene dried Christ's feet with her hair. This gesture of abnegation became a pagan symbol in Marlene's adventurous life.

She became a close friend of my wife, Tatiana. She called her "my sister," sent her a photograph of herself inscribed *"Tatiana, je vous aime."* They became inseparable. When Marlene lay in Presbyterian Hospital at the far northern end of the city, Tatiana visited her every day for three weeks, bringing her love and anything she craved. We saw a great deal of her. Sometimes when I was ill, sick with ulcers, she would cook for me her panacea, a special chicken soup or beef tea. When she lived with the great Jean Gabin she learned hearty French peasant dishes, her favorite being a boiled beef *à la ficelle* in a huge pot. Beef cut in chunks would be tied with string; at the table, everyone could pull out pieces by pulling on the strings hanging outside the pot. The contrast with the public Marlene, whose every simple gesture epitomized a legend, was a constant bewilderment.

Her Lola-Lola, her theatrical personality, was an erotic, liberated, power-loose woman. She behaved then as if she were above all constraints. Her handling of the tubular mike onstage when she sang "Johnny" was a daring, provocative evocation of the love act. When she faced an audience, she seemed to spit out her scorn. For her, I believe, performance became a challenge to subdue and finally bring to an orgasmic enthusiasm a spellbound, vanquished audience. After it was over, of course, she had to escape the ever-dangerous overenthusiastic pawing; everyone wanted to touch her. To experience getting away with her after one of these performances was unforgettable.

Perhaps the most tangible dangers were actually onstage. The hazards of being the star became manifest one evening while she was on tour in Australia. The famous gown was literally sewn on her body, tight as a second skin, so she could walk only with difficulty. As she bowed to the thunderous applause, her foot caught in the upswing of the curtain and she was thrown across the stage. The injuries she suffered were so grave she felt that only Dr. DeBakey could save her. She never fully recovered.

To share everyday life with a legend of glamour one has quickly to forget the cliché in one's mind and get used to observing a human presence. When she let us be her friends, she became natural and open. Often she would wear no makeup. Her skin, so pale and white, had a translucent quality.

It became fun to discuss things with her and ask her opinions. She would make provocative pronouncements in her slightly tinged-with-German English. One came to feel that these categorical statements, even if wrong or silly, were endowed with an intuition given only to some women. In spite of her ultrafeminine trappings, she behaved with the brusque, almost weary indifference usually claimed only by men. Yet in her inner life she was a conservative. She treated modern art with disdain, loving art that brought her a decorative peace, preferring the tradition of the established.

Marlene adored her grandchildren and was a dream grandmother. But she was an actress, and even when playing with them, she exuded a seething excess of joy and engagement. She assumed the needed role at every moment. Christmas with Marlene was an orgy of giving. One present was never enough, and each gift was lavishly, oversplendidly wrapped in special rare papers and elaborate ribbons, even lace. Christmas metamorphosed into a competition to see who could be the most generous and imaginative. The mountain of gifts under the tree became too much to endure. Marlene's anguish of inadequacy, her constant inner fear of somehow failing to show her love, expressed itself in these extravagant gestures. She gave of things and of herself. At times she smothered with her generosity, but even this reminded us of a life larger than nature, an abundance that only a myth could yield.

What makes some women so extraordinarily photogenic? When I was alone with Marlene, photographing her, I was struck by her knowledge of light, her lifelong romance with the camera. As I was taking the pictures I realized that whichever way she turned, she looked great. There was no need for her to pose. Her features did not seem so extraordinary in real life; they hungered for light. In her Prussian face, I believe, the bone structure, with its trace of faraway Mongol ancestry, was the dominant feature, enhanced by that light-grabbing skin. Makeup can only intensify these God-given wonders, not create them.

Onscreen or onstage her face became a motionless mask, an unchanging image imprinted on the world's imagination. We, the public, need immobility to fix forever in our dreams the object of our desire. When I was with her I was awed by the seemingly miraculous transformation of her perhaps unexceptional presence into a spellbinding icon. She told me that there was one particular lighting expert she hoped would work with her in each of her films. He knew exactly how to project the spotlight so that the shadow under her nose would glorify and refine her mask. I also believe that often she would create an amorous relationship with all involved in her films—director, leading man, and even the cameramen. She had a logical theory: if the professional men around her admired, loved, and desired her, they would be compelled to enhance and intensify her image.

I am afraid that she was rarely, if ever, off guard. She was, of course, constantly at the mercy of photographers, me included. She trusted me, so with me she was intimate and relaxed; but one sensed beneath her "naturalness" a deep awareness of her projected image. She would willingly play the photographer's game, lending herself easily to new suggestions that intrigued her and falling into the spirit of experimentation. But she seemed to know in advance what the results would be. I did not ask her to blow smoke. With her visual imagination and inventiveness, she knew, seeing the black background, what would be her most effective contribution to the sitting. The cigarette was for many years a magical prop for gesture. The fashion models, the photographers, liked the pretext of smoking as a stylization of modernism. The woman smoking with casual indifference appeared liberated, more secure and sure of herself. For Marlene, in her man's suit or tails, it enriched still more her ambiguous, suggestive stance. She loved to light the cigarettes of her women friends. Perhaps she dared these knowing, seductive hints at male-female interplay out of spite that such actions were acceptable only for men. Smoking, her need and passion, a sign of her toughness and liberation, also became an opportunity for her to play. The patterns of smoke blowing into the air created a surprising poetic illusion.

For all the glamour and polish of her clothes and makeup, her hands had a naturalness that surprised. They were the humble working hands of a housewife and grandmother. Throughout her life she used this humbleness as a weapon of control. She often kissed the hands of a man or woman as a gesture of submission from one they so admired. In this way she would further draw them under her spell. Once, in Russia, she knelt on the stage to show her boundless respect for a writer.

An author who had stamped her for life was Knut Hamsun, whose noble, earthy humanity fit with many of Marlene's moods. And Hemingway, with his staccato dialogue, this he-man writer of tales, appealed to her masculine will. Wherever she traveled, in every dressing room she would pin his portrait, an icon calling for a great performance, as if, like the torero in a bullfight, she had to be sublime or die. This courageous side of her nature predominated. She rejected Hitler and threw herself body, voice, and soul into the Allied cause.

The intensity of her friendships, of her love and passion, knew no bounds. She would not tolerate any weakness in response to her heroic ideals. In all realms she regally dismissed the unimportant, whether people or troubling thoughts. She enjoyed control; but, disciplined and punctual, she was a severe master to herself as well. Hers was an uplifting and demanding standard of behavior. Many who knew her found it exhausting. The few who survived her tests were initiated into a spiritual, colorful, and unexpected understanding of life's possibilities.

Marlene, to us you revealed a great deal that the screen camouflaged. I have so much to say to you and about you, but somehow I feel that not too much should be said. There is a mystery about you that is a vital part of your captivating power. Thank you, Marlene, for being more than yourself. Thank you forever, beloved Marlene, for not settling for half measures. With you it was always all or nothing. You gambled, you played with chance, with luck. Your talent had a throwaway dash, a devil-may-care roughness. Life is tough, but one has to lick it and survive. You survived and won!

—ALEXANDER LIBERMAN

Don't cry

for me '

THE OTHER

Marlene

Marlene

OFF GUARD

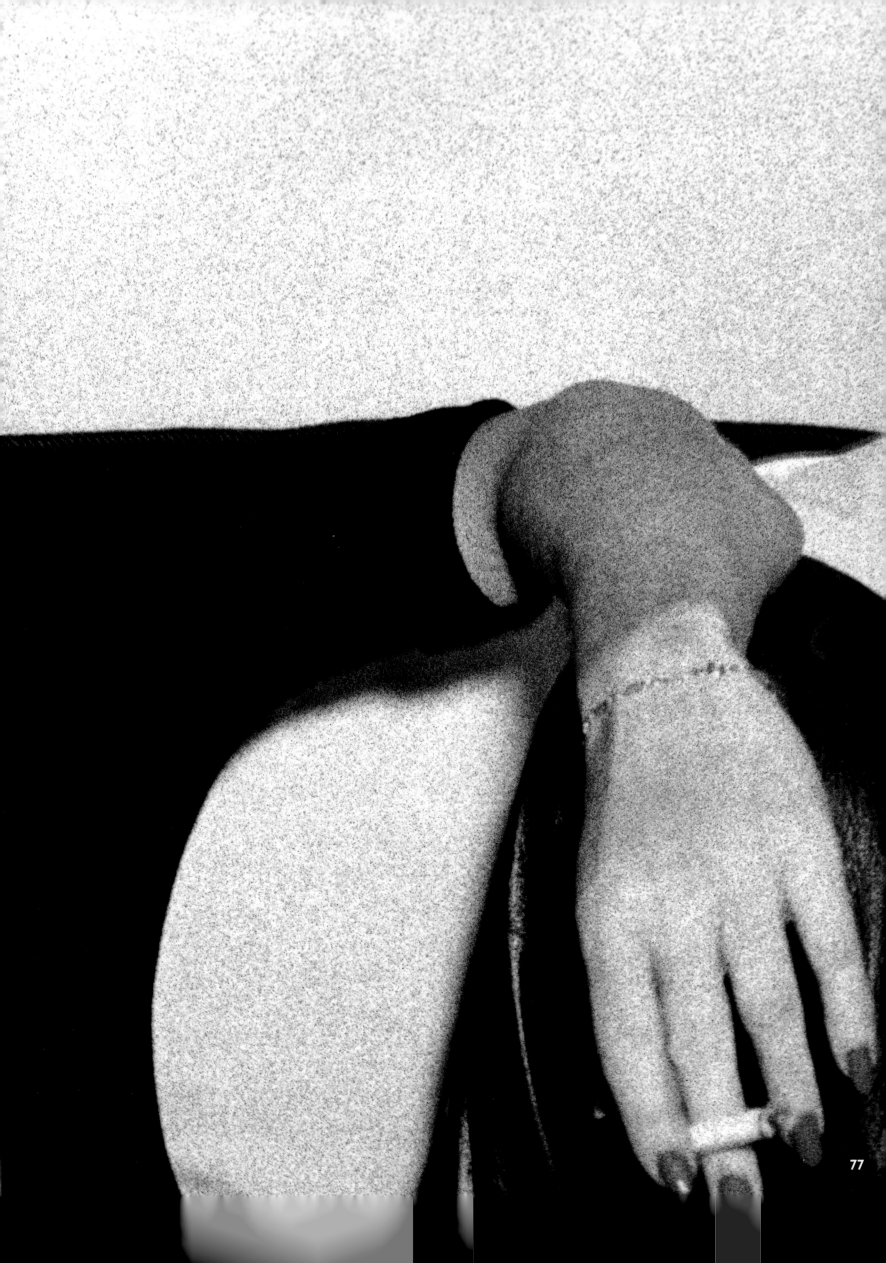

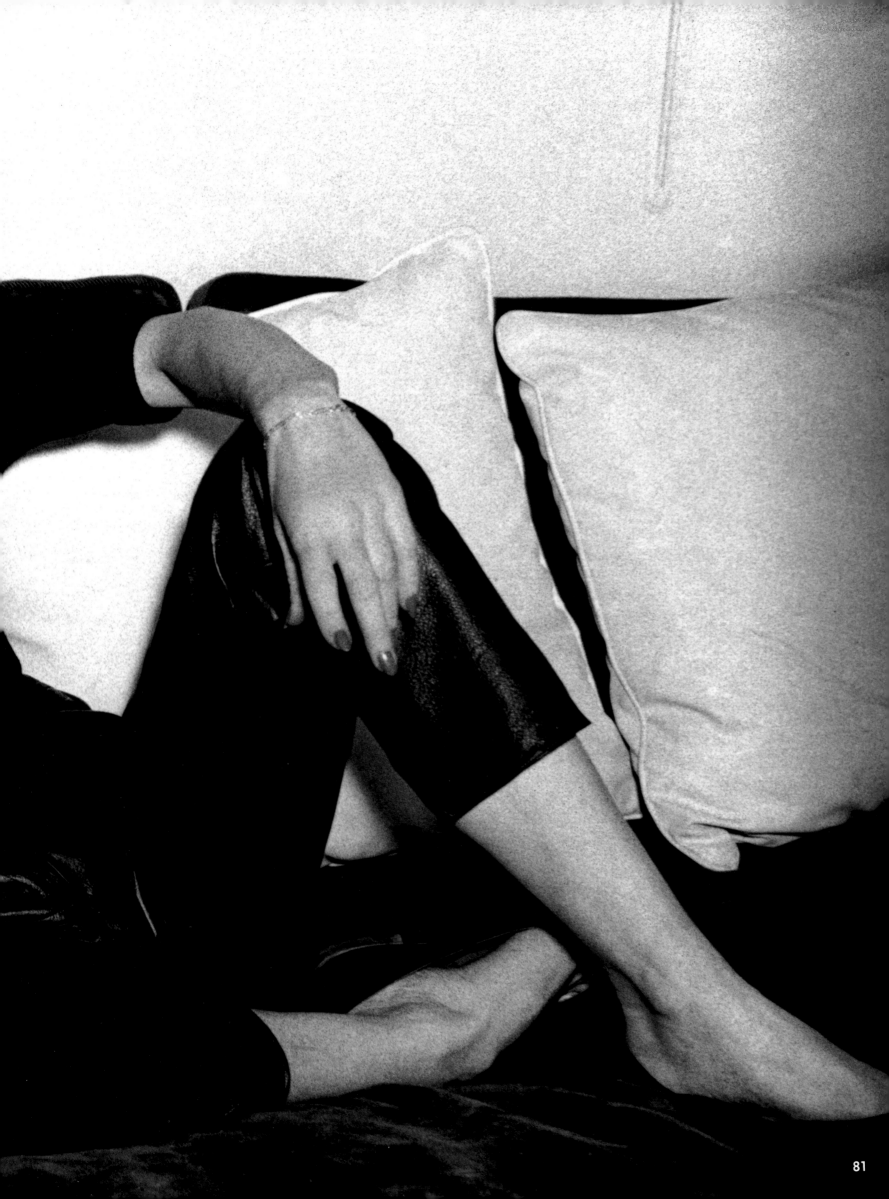

Marlene ON STAGE

LILLI MARLENE

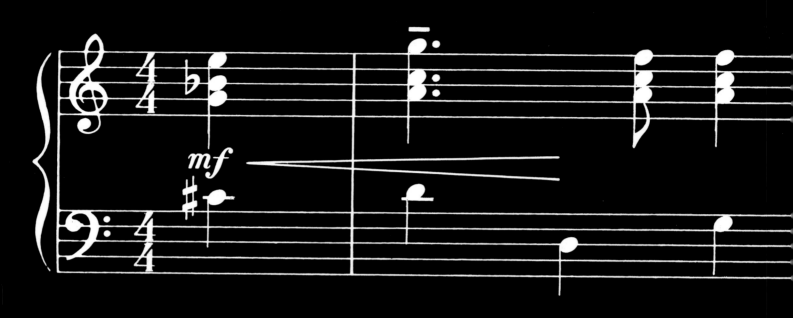

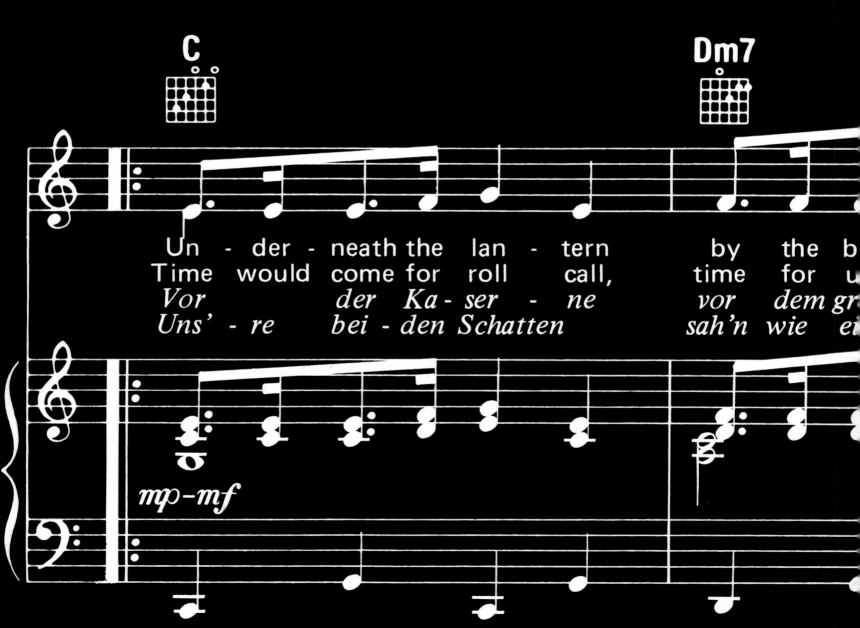

Un - der - neath the lan - tern by the b
Time would come for roll call, time for u
Vor der Ka - ser - ne vor dem gr
Uns' - re bei - den Schatten sah'n wie ei

English Lyric by TOMMIE CONNOR
Music by NORBERT SCHULTZE

G7

rack gate,	Dar - ling I re - mem - ber the
to part,	Dar - ling I'd ca - ress you and
en Tor	*stand ei - ne La - ter - ne und*
her aus;	*dass wir so lieb was hat - ten*

I kiss you
from afar –

Marlene

Marlene

THE
LIFE

CHRONOLOGY

1901   Born, Maria Magdalena Dietrich, Berlin, December 27

1924   Married Rudolf Sieber

1925   Daughter, Maria, born

1930   Lola-Lola in *The Blue Angel* (Erich Pommer/UFA, directed by Josef von Sternberg)

       Amy Jolly in *Morocco* (Paramount, directed by Josef von Sternberg)

1931   X27 in *Dishonored* (Paramount, directed by Josef von Sternberg)

1932   Shanghai Lily in *Shanghai Express* (Paramount, directed by Josef von Sternberg)

       Helen Faraday in *Blonde Venus* (Paramount, directed by Josef von Sternberg)

1933   Lily Czepanek in *Song of Songs* (Paramount, directed by Rouben Mamoulian)

1934   Catherine the Great in *The Scarlet Empress* (Paramount, directed by Josef von Sternberg)

1935   Concha Perez in *The Devil Is a Woman* (Paramount, directed by Josef von Sternberg)

1936   Madeleine de Beaupré in *Desire* (Paramount, directed by Frank Borzage)

       Domini Enfilden in *The Garden of Allah* (Selznick-International, directed by Richard Boleslawski)

1937   Alexandra in *Knight Without Armor* (Produced by Alexander Korda, directed by Jacques Feyder)

       Maria Barker in *Angel* (Paramount, directed by Ernst Lubitsch)

1939   Frenchy in *Destry Rides Again* (Universal Pictures, directed by George Marshall)

1940   Bijou in *Seven Sinners* (Universal Pictures, directed by Tay Garnett)

1941   Clair Ledoux in *The Flame of New Orleans* (Universal Pictures, directed by René Clair)

       Fay Duval in *Manpower* (Warner Bros.–First National, directed by Raoul Walsh)

1942   Elizabeth Madden in *The Lady Is Willing* (Columbia Pictures, directed by Mitchell Leisen)

       Cherry Mallotte in *The Spoilers* (Universal Pictures, directed by Ray Enright)

       Josie Winters in *Pittsburgh* (Universal Pictures, directed by Lewis Seiler)

Preceding page, an early picture with von Sternberg, her discoverer and lover.

1944   Appeared in *Follow the Boys* (Universal Pictures, directed by Eddie Sutherland)

        Jamilla in *Kismet* (MGM, directed by William Dieterle)

        European USO tour

1946   Blanche Ferrand in *Martin Roumagnac* (Alcina, directed by Georges Lacombe)

1947   Lydia in *Golden Earrings* (Paramount, directed by Mitchell Leisen)

1948   Erika von Schluetow in *A Foreign Affair* (Paramount, directed by Billy Wilder)

1949   Appeared in *Jigsaw* (Tower Pictures, directed by Fletcher Markle)

1950   Charlotte Inwood in *Stage Fright* (Warner Bros.–First National, directed by
        Alfred Hitchcock)

1951   Monica Teasdale in *No Highway in the Sky* (20th Century-Fox, directed by Henry Koster)

1952   Altar Keane in *Rancho Notorious* (Fidelity Pictures, directed by Fritz Lang)

1956   Appeared in *Around the World in Eighty Days* (Michael Todd Company, Inc.,
        directed by Michael Anderson)

1957   Marquise Maria de Crèvecoeur in *The Monte Carlo Story* (Titanus, directed
        by Samuel A. Taylor)

        Christine Vole in *Witness for the Prosecution* (Edward Small–Arthur Hornblow,
        directed by Billy Wilder)

1958   Appeared in *Touch of Evil* (Universal-International, directed by Orson Welles)

1960   Toured Germany and Israel

1961   Mme. Bertholt in *Judgment at Nuremberg* (Roxlom, directed by Stanley Kramer)

1962   Narrated *The Black Fox*, documentary on Hitler (Arthur Steloff–Image,
        directed by Louis Clyde Stoumen)

1964   Appeared in *Paris When It Sizzles* (Paramount, directed by Richard Quine)

        Toured Russia

1978   Baroness von Semering in *Just a Gigolo* (Leguan , directed by David Hemmings)

1981   Retired to 12 avenue Montaigne in Paris

1984   *Marlene*, a documentary biography (Zev Braun, directed by Maximilian Schell)

1992   Died, in Paris, May 6. Buried in the Friedenau Cemetery in Berlin, next to her mother's grave.

PHOTOGRAPHS BY ALEXANDER LIBERMAN

Following pages: 119, *Blonde Venus*, 1932; 120, *The Scarlet Empress*, 1934.